Peter Pindar

A Complimentary Epistle to James Bruce, Esq., the Abyssinian Traveller

Third Edition

Peter Pindar

A Complimentary Epistle to James Bruce, Esq., the Abyssinian Traveller
Third Edition

ISBN/EAN: 9783337209391

Printed in Europe, USA, Canada, Australia, Japan

Cover: Foto ©Andreas Hilbeck / pixelio.de

More available books at **www.hansebooks.com**

A COMPLIMENTARY EPISTLE

TO

JAMES BRUCE, Esq.

THE ABYSSINIAN TRAVELLER:

By PETER PINDAR Esq.

———— *Non Fabula mendax.*
WONDERS!—WONDERS!!—WONDERS!!!

THE THIRD EDITION.

LONDON:
Printed for G. KEARSLEY, Fleet-Street. MDCCXC.

[Entered at Stationers' Hall.]

PRICE TWO SHILLINGS AND SIX-PENCE.

EPISTLE DEDICATORY.

ILLUSTRIOUS SIR,

PERMIT a poor son of Apollo to make an offering of his Pamphlet (a sort of widow's mite), for the pleasure received from your five quartos. Aware of the dangers of launching into the foaming sea of usual dedication, in which many an unfortunate author has been drowned, I tremble at my present attempt. Exalted panegyric too frequently incurs the suspicion of a sneer. *Your* dedication, illustrious Sir, to the best of kings, strikes me as the most perfect model of imitation—it is a column of Attic elegance and simplicity, erected to a deserving monarch. Pray, Sir, did his august Majesty honour it with a perusal before publication? It truly forms the *ne plus ultra* of human panegyric; and what is marvellous, cannot be suspected of adulation. Pray, Sir, how much might his Majesty give you for it?

What a similarity, illustrious Sir, between yourself and Mr. JAMES BOSWELL; and yet what a distance! Both gloriously ambitious, both great scholars, both intellectually adorned, both popular gentlemen, both dealers in history, and both descended from kings! But Mr. JAMES BOSWELL's ambition was not of so bold a wing as yours. *He* was content with a journey to Scotland, to exhibit Dr. SAMUEL JOHNSON, the Lexicographer, to the *literati* of that country. *Your* more exalted ideas could only be satisfied with a display of the head quarters of the IMMORTAL

NILE,

Nile, who had puzzled the purfuits of men for feven thoufand years. Whilft Mr. Boswell entertains only with a breakfaft on fpaldings (*alias* dried whitings), the fublimer Bruce treats us with a difh of lion. Whilft Boswell brings us acquainted with plain Scottifh gentlewomen only, the gallant Bruce charms us with romantic tales of Queen Sittinia, &c. Whilft Mr. Boswell prefents us only with an anecdote of a flannel night-cap, made by Mifs M'Leod, for the Doctor's bald head; the fublimer Bruce tells of a piece of fatin, and fix handfome crimfon and green handkerchiefs, moft gallantly tranfmitted to the beautiful Aiscach, of Teawa. Whilft Mr. Boswell amufes us only with his drunken bout, and confequently a fimple emetic fcene, the foaring Bruce greets us with the more important hiftory of a thundering Diarrhæa. Whilft Mr. Boswell prides himfelf only upon his defcent from a Scottifh King, the penetrating Bruce difcovers an origin from King Solomon and the Queen of Sheba; which, under the rofe, muft be eftablifhing a baftardy in the family, as the Abyffinian Queen could be nothing more than Solomon's concubine, their marriage having never been proved.

Pray, Sir, what may his Majefty intend to do with your invalable Drawings, &c. &c.? Are they to be engraved, *pro bono publico*, at the expence of the royal purfe; or kept *cautioufly* locked up in a drawer at Buckingham-houfe, to induce the *dilettanti* to figh for the publication? Poffibly they are deftined to be a pofthumous work of the greateft of Kings; but not like pofthumous works in general, to difgrace the dead.

I am, Illustrious Sir,

P. P.

A COMPLIMENTARY EPISTLE.

SWEET is the tale, however strange its air,
That bids the public eye *astonied* stare!
Sweet is the tale, howe'er uncouth its shape,
That makes the world's wide mouth with wonder gape!
Behold our infancies in tales delight,
That bolt like hedgehog quills the hair upright
Of ghosts how pleas'd is ev'ry child to hear!
To such is Jack the giant-killer dear!

Dread monsters issuing from the flame or flood,

Charm, tho' with horror cloath'd they chill the blood!

What makes a tale so sleepy, languid, dull?

Things as they happened—not of marvel full.

What gives a zest, and keeps alive attention?

A tale that wears the visage of invention:

A tale of lions, spectres, shipwreck, thunder;

A wonder, or first cousin to a wonder.

Mysterious conduct! yet 'tis Nature's plan

To sow with wonder's seeds the soul of man,

That ev'ry where in sweet profusion rise,

And sprout luxuriant through the mouth and eyes!

What to the *vasty* deep * Sir Joseph gave,

As of the world, the sport of wind and wave?

* Sir Joseph Banks.

What bade the Knight amid thofe fcenes remote,

Sleep with Queen Oborea in the boat?

What unconfounded leap to Newton's chair?

What, but to make a world with wonder ftare?

What bids a ----- on Wimbledon, Blackheath,

So oft rejoice the regiments of death;

While Britain's mightier bulwark flighted lies,

And vainly groaning for its Cæfar fighs?

What with the vulgar pigs of Afcot taken,

Devour on Afcot-heath his annual bacon?

What bade that great, great man, a goodly fight,

Watch his wife's di'mond petticoat all night;

And what that wife of great, great, great renown,

Make her own caps, and darn a thread-bare gown?

What bade the charming * LADY MARY fly

MARCHESI's squeeze for PACCHIEROTTI's sigh?

What MASTER EDGECUMBE deal in rhiming ware?

What, but to put all ‡ Cawsand in a stare?

Sweet child of verse, who with importance big,

Pleas'd its own self, and eterniz'd a pig; †

Whilst mad an equal weight of praise to share,

OLD MOUNT plays Punchenello to a hair.

What makes a girl the shops for novels rove?

The sweet impossibilities of love;

---

* Lady Mary Duncan.

‡ A small fishing town near Mount Edgecumbe.

† This pig, Cupid, who many years ago fell in love with the Earl, has a monument erected to his memory, with an inscription on it by Lord Valletort, the Earl's son.— It is said, that His Majesty, when at Mount Edgecumbe, happening to be gravely pondering near his grave, the Queen, who was at some distance, asked him, what he was looking at so seriously. His Majesty, with a great deal of humour, immediately replied, "The family vault, Charly; family vault, family vault."

Quixotic

Quixotic deeds to catch the flying fair;

To pant at dangers, and at marvels stare.

What prompteth Chloe, conscious of the charms

That croud the souls of swains with wild alarms,

To give the swelling bosom's milk-white skin

A veil of gauze so marveloufly thin?

What but a kind intention of the fair

To treat the eyes of shepherds with a stare?

Behold! Religion's self, celestial dame,

Founds on the rock of miracle her fame:

A sacred building, that defies decay,

That sin's wild waves can never wash away!

What made *John Rolle (except for Exon's stare)

Drill-serjeant to the aldermen and may'r;

E'er

---

* Mr. John Rolle's dread of a failure in the *etiquette* of presentment to his Majesty when at Exeter, prevailed on him to take a deal of trouble with gentlemen who were

E'er from the hall he led his chosen bands,

To view the KING OF NATIONS, and kiss hands?

How rarely man the haunts of wisdom seeks,

Pleas'd with the life of cabbages and leeks!

Tho' form'd to plough the soil, divinely strong,

'Tis famine goads him, like an ox, along:

But BRUCE, on *curiosity*'s wild wings,

Darts, hawk-like, where the game of marvel springs.

Let envy kindle with the blush of shame,

That dares to call thee, BRUCE, a thief of fame.

were to be introduced at the *Levee :* but, in spite of all his intellectual powers, which, like his corporeal, are of more than ordinary texture, much disorder happened; indeed the best of kings was three or four times nearly overturned. Many were the gentlemen that Mr. ROLLE was forced to place himself behind, to pull down properly on their knees; and many were the gentlemen he was obliged to run after, and make face to the right about, who uncourteously, though unwittingly, in quitting the presence, had turned their unpolished tails on majesty.

Pleas'd

Pleas'd to thy wonder's vortex to be drawn,
A thousand volumes could not make me yawn:
And (O accept a salutary hint)—
The world will read as fast as thou canst print.

Curs'd by the goose's and the critic's quill,
What tortures tear us, and what horrors thrill!
Thus that small imp, a tooth, a simple bone,
Can make fair ladies and great heroes groan;
Tear hopeless virgins from their happy dream,
And bid for doctors 'stead of sweethearts scream;
In tears the tender tossing infant steep,
And from its eyelids brush the dews of sleep;
Where, with a cheek in cherub blushes drest,
It seeks, with fruitless cries, its vanish'd rest.
Far diff'rent, THOU, erect in conscious pride,
Colossal dar'st the critic host bestride;

Like yelping coward curs canſt make them ſkip,
And tremble at the thunder of thy whip.

How hard that thou, a buſy working bee,
Shouldſt range from flow'r to flow'r, from tree to tree;
Fly loaded home from ſhrubs of richeſt prime,
Egyptian, Nubian, Abyſſinian thyme,
And plund'ring * drones upon thine honey thrive,
Who never gave an atom to the hive!
Huge WHALE of marvel-hunters, further ſay,
And glad the preſent and the future day;
Speak! did no angel, proud to intervene,
Bear thee, like Habbakuk, from ſcene to ſcene?

Lo! moon-ey'd Wonder opes her lap to thee:
How niggardly, alas! to luckleſs me!

* Alluding to an Abridgement of Mr. Bruce's Travels.

Where'er

Where'er through trackless woods thy luckier way,
Marvels, like dew-drops, beam on ev'ry spray.
Blest man! whate'er thou wishest to behold,
Nature as strongly wishes to unfold;
Of all her wardrobe offers every rag,
Of which thy skill hath form'd a conj'ror's bag.
Thy deeds are giants, covering ours with shame!
Poor wasted pigmies! skeletons of fame!
To thee how kindly hath thy genius giv'n
The massy keys of yonder star-clad heav'n;
With leave, whene'er thou wishest to unlock it,
To put a few eclipses in thy pocket!
Nature, where'er thou tread'st, exalts her form;
The whisp'ring zephyr swells a howling storm;
Where pebbles lay, and riv'lets purl'd before,
Huge promontories rise, and oceans roar.

Thrice envy'd man (if truth each volume sings),

Thy life how happy! hand and glove with kings!

A simple swain, a stranger to a throne,

I ne'er sat down with kings to pick a bone!

For smiles I gap'd not, crouch'd not for assistance;

But paid my salutations at a distance:

Yet live, O KINGS, to see a distant date,

Because I've got a pretty good estate;

A comely spot near Helicon, that thrives;

A leasehold tho', that hangs upon their lives;

Set to GEORGE KEARSLEY, at a moderate rent;

Enough for me, poor swain, it brings content.

Were heav'n to place a crown upon my head,

So meek, so modest, I should faint with dread;

And like some honest bishop, with a sigh,

" Pity my greatness, Lord!" would be my cry.

Poets, like spiders, now-a-days must spin,

E'en from *themselves*, the threads of life so thin.

Nought pleaseth now the rulers of great nations,

But books of wonders, and sweet dedications.

Kings, like the mountains of the moon, indeed,

Proud of their stature, lift a lofty head;

Heads, like the mountains also, cold and raw,

That, ice-envelop'd, seldom feel a thaw.

O may the worst of ills my soul betide,

For *me* if ever love-sick lady dy'd!

If fatal darts from these two eyes of mine,

Play'd havock with fair ladies hearts, like thine:

No, no! I ever a hard bargain drove,

And purchas'd ev'ry atom of my love.

O BRUCE.

O Bruce, I own, all candour, that I look
With envy, downright envy, on thy book;
A book like Pfalmanazar's, form'd to laſt,
That gives th' hiſtoric eye a fweet repaſt;
A book like Mandeville's, that yields delight,
And puts poor probability to flight;
A book that e'en Pontopidan would own;
A book moſt humbly offered to the throne;
A book, how happy, which the King of Iſles
Admires (fays rumour), and receiv'd with fmiles!

The fool, with equal gape, aſtoniſh'd fees,
Through Wonder's glaſſes, elephants, and fleas;
But thou, in Wonder's fchool long bred, full grown,
Art pleas'd indeed with elephants alone:

Hadſt

Hadſt thou been GOD, an inſult to thy ſight,
Thy majeſty had ſcorn'd to make a mite.

Know, where th' Atlantic holds th' unwieldy whale,
My heart had panted at the monſter's tail:
Had BRUCE been there, th' invincible, the brave,
How had he daſh'd at once beneath the wave!
Bold with his dirk the mighty fiſh purſu'd,
And ſtain'd whole leagues of ocean with his blood.
Then riſing glorious from the great attack,
Grac'd with the wat'ry tyrant on his back!

'Mid thoſe fair * iſles, the happy iſles of old,
Plains that the ghoſts of kings and chiefs patrol'd,

---

* The Canaries, or the Inſulæ Fortunatæ of the Ancients.

These eyes have seen; but, let me truth confess,
No royal spectre came these eyes to bless:
To no one chieftain-phantom too, I vow,
With rev'rence, did I ever make my bow:
Gone to make room, poor ghosts, so Fate inclines,
For gangs of lazy Spaniards and their vines.
But had thy foot, illustrious Trav'ller, trod,
Like me, the precincts of th' Elysian sod;
Full of enquiry, easy, unconfounded,
By spectres hadst thou quickly been surrounded;
Then had we heard thy book of wonder boast,
How BRUCE the brave shook hands with ev'ry ghost!
In vain did I phœnomena pursue,
For Wonder waits upon the chosen few.

Whate'er

Whate'er I saw requir'd no witch's storm—

Slight deeds, that nature could with ease perform!

Audacious, to purloin my flesh and fish,

No golden eagles hopp'd into my dish.

Nor crocodiles, by love of knowledge led,

To mark my figure, left their oozy bed;

Nor loaded camels, to provoke my stare,

Sublimely whirl'd, like straws, amid the air;

Nor, happy in a stomach form'd of steel,

On roaring lions have I made a meal.

Unequal *mine* with lions' bones to cope;

Thy jaws can only on such viands ope.

O hadst thou trod, like me, the happy isle,

Whose * mountain treats all mountains with a smile;

* Teneriffe.

Bold

Bold hadst thou climb'd th' ascent, an easy matter,

And, nobly daring, sous'd into the *crater;*

Then out agen hadst vaulted with a hop,

Quick as a sweeper from a chimney top.

O had thy curious eye beheld, like mine,

The * isle which glads the heart with richest wine!

Beneath its vines, with common clusters crown'd,

At eve my wand'ring steps a passage found,

Where rose the hut, and neither rich nor poor,

The wife and husband, seated at the door,

Touch'd, when the labours of the day were done,

The wire of music to the setting sun;

Where, blest, a tender offspring, ranged around,

Join'd their small voices to the silver sound.

* Madeira.

But had *thine* eye this simple scene explor'd,

The man at once had sprung a sceptre'd lord;

Princes and princesses the *bearns* had been;

The hut a palace, and the wife a queen;

Their golden harps had ravish'd thy two ears,

And beggar'd all the music of the spheres;

So kind is nature always pleas'd to be,

When visited by favourites, like *thee!*

Strange! thou hast seen the land, that, to its shame,

Ne'er heard our good -----'s virtues nor his name!

I've only seen those regions, let me say,

Where his great *virtues* never found their way.

   Alas, I never met with royal scenes!

No vomits gave to Abyssinian queens!

                           Drew

Drew not from royal arms the purple tide,

Nor scotch'd with fleams, a sceptre'd lady's hide;

Nor, in anatomy so very stout,

Ventur'd to turn a princess inside out;

Nor, blushing, stripp'd me to the very skin,

To give a royal blackamoor a grin.

I never saw (with ignorance I own)

Mule-mounted monarchs seek th' imperial throne;

Which mule the carpet spoil'd—a dirty beast!

First stal'd; then—What?—Oblivion cloud the rest.

I saw no king, whose subjects form'd a riot,

And, imp-like, howl'd around him for his quiet.

Nor have I been where men (what loss, alas!)

Kill half a cow, and turn the rest to grass.

Where'er,

Where'er, great Trav'ller, thou art pleas'd to tread,

The teeming skies rain wonders on thy head:

No common birth to greet thine eye appears,

But sacred labours of a thousand years.

Where'er the Nile shall pour the smallest sluice,

The rills shall curl into the name of BRUCE.

And, lo! a universe his praise shall utter,

Who, first of mortals, found her parent gutter.

And, let me add, of gutters too the QUEEN,

Without whose womb the Nile had never been.

Thus many a man, whose deeds have made a pother,

Has had a scurvy father or a mother.

O form'd in art and science to surpass;

To whom e'en VALOUR is an arrant ass;

O BRUCE,

O Bruce, moſt ſurely Travel's eldeſt ſon;

Tell, prithee, all that thou haſt ſeen and done!

I fear thou hideſt half thy feats, unkind;

A thouſand wonders, ah! remain behind!

Where is the chariot-wheel with Pharoah's name,

Fiſh'd from the old Red Sea to ſwell thy fame?

Where the horſe-ſhoe with Pharoah's arms, and found

Where wicked Pharoah and his hoſt were drown'd?

Where of that ſtone a ſlice, and freſh account,

Giv'n by the Lord to Moses on the Mount?

And where a ſlice of that ſtone's elder brother,

That, broken, forc'd th' All-Wise t' engrave another?

Where of the cradle too, a ſacred ruſh?

Where a true charcoal of the burning buſh?

And

And O the jewel, curious gem, disclose,

That dangled from the Queen of Sheba's nose,

When, with hard questions, and two roguish eyes,

She rode to puzzle Solomon the Wise?

Sagacious Terrier in Discovery's mine,

Shall Nature form no more a nose like thine?

No more display'd the pearls of wonder beam,

When thou, great man, art past the Stygian stream?

To Afric wilt thou never, Bruce, return?

Howl, Britain! Europe, Abyssinia mourn!

Droop shall Discovery's wing, her bosom sigh,

And Marvel meet no more the ravish'd eye;

Nature outstep her modesty no more;

Her cataracts of wonder cease to roar,

Forc'd to a common channel to subside,
And pour no longer an astounding tide?
O bid not yet thy lucky labours cease;
Still let the Land of Wonder feel increase:
Thy loads of dung, delightful ordure, yield,
And blossom with fertility the field:
Gates, hedges mend, that Ignorance pull'd down,
And bring in triumph back each kidnapp'd town.
Though Envy damns thy volumes of surprise,
Blest I devour them with unsated eyes!
What tho' sour JOHNSON cry'd, with cynic sneer,
" I deem'd at first, indeed, BRUCE had been there:
" But soon the eye of keen investigation,
" Prov'd all the fellow's tale a fabrication."

But

But who, alas! on Johnson's word relies,

Who saw the too kind North with jaundice'd eyes;

Who rode to Hawthornden's fair scene by night,

For fear a Scottish tree might wound his sight;

And bent from decent candour to depart,

Allow'd a Scotchman neither head nor heart?

Grant fiction half thy volumes of surprise,

High in the scale of merit shalt thou rise:

Still to Fame's temple dost thou boast pretension;

For thine the *rara avis* of invention!

And, lo! amidst thy work of lab'ring years,

A dignity of egotism appears;

A stile that classic authors should pursue;

A stile that peerless * Katerfelto knew!

Thou

---

* A late celebrated Philosopher and Conjuror.

Thou dear man-mountain of discovery, run;

Again attempt an Abyssinian fun!

Yes go; a second journey, BRUCE, pursue;

More volumes of rich hist'ry bring to view.

O run ere Time the spectred tombs invade,

And seize the crumbling wonders from the shade;

Croud with fair columns, struck by Time, thy page,

And snatch the falling grandeur from his rage:

Give that old Time a vomit too, and draw

More of Egyptian marvels from his maw;

Bid him disgorge (by moderns call'd *a hum*)

Scratch'd by ten thousand trav'llers, Memnon's bum;

And, what all rarities must needs surpass,

The tail, the curious tail, of Balaam's ass.

Say,

Say, what should stop, O BRUCE, thy grand career;

Of Fame the fav'rite, and no child of Fear?

DANGER's huge form, so dread to vulgar eyes,

Pants at thy presence, and a coward flies.

Where other trav'llers, fraught with terror, roam,

Lo! BRUCE in Wonder-Land is quite at home;

The same cool eye on Nature's forms looks down;

Lions and rats, the courtier and the clown.

Whate'er thine action, wonder crouds the tale;

It smells of Brobdignag—it boasts a scale!

Fond of the lofty, BRUCE no pigmy loves—

Who likes a pigmy that a giant moves?

Again—what pigmy, with a form of lath,

Lost in his shadow, likes the MAN OF GATH?

The bowerly hoſteſs, for a cart-horſe fit,
Scorns DAPHNE's reed-like ſhape, and calls her *chit*;
Whilſt on the rough *robuſtious* lump of Nature,
Contemptuous DAPHNE whiſpers "What a creature!"
Pity! purſuits like thine ſhould feel a pauſe,
More than half ſmother'd by fair Fame's applauſe!
I ſee thee ſafe return'd from MARVEL's mine,
Whoſe gems in ev'ry rock ſo precious ſhine;
Proud of the product of a world unknown,
Unloading all thy treaſure at the throne;
While courtiers cry aloud with one accord,
"Moſt marv'lous is the reign of George the Third!"
How like the butchers' boys we ſometimes meet,
Stuck round with bladders, in a London ſtreet:

In full-blown majesty who move, and drop

The bloated burthen in an OILMAN's shop;

Whilst country bumpkins, gazing at the door,

Cry they " *ne'er zeed zo vine a zight bevore.*"

I see old NILE, the king of floods, arise,

Shake hands, and welcome thee with happy eyes;

Otters and alligators in his train,

Made by thy five immortal volumes vain;

Weasels and polecats, sheregrigs, carrion-crows,

Seen and smelt only by thine eyes and nose.

" Son of the Arts, and Cousin of a King,

" Loud as a kettle-drum whose actions ring,"

Exclaims the king of floods, " thy books I've read,

" And for thy birth-place, envy Brother TWEED."

O BRUCE

O Bruce, by Fame for ever to be sung;

Job's war-horse fierce, thy neck with thunder hung:

When envious Death shall put thee in his stable,

Snipp'd life's fine thread, that should have been a cable;

Lo! to thy mem'ry shall the marble swell,

Mausoleum huge, and all thy actions tell!

Here in fair sculpture, the recording stones

Shall give thee glorious, cracking lions' bones;

There, which the squeamish souls of Britain shocks,

Rich steaks devouring from the living ox;

Here, staring on thee from the realm of water,

Full many a virtuoso alligator;

There, Bruce informing queens, in naked pride,

The feel and colour of a Scotsman's hide;

Here

Here of the genealogy a tree,
Branching from Solomon's wife trunk to thee:
There, with a valour nought could dare withstand,
Bruce fighting an hyæna hand to hand;
Which dread hyæna (what a beast uncouth!)
Fought with a pound of candles in his mouth:
Here temples bursting glorious on the view,
Which Hist'ry, tho' a gossip, never knew:
There columns starting from the earth and flood,
Just like the razor-fish from sand and mud;
Here a wise Monarch with voracious looks,
Receiving all thy drawings and thy books;
Whilst Fame behind him all so solemn sings
The lib'ral spirit of the best of kings.

Man says, O BRUCE, that thou wert hardly us'd;
That our great king at first thy book refus'd;
Indeed look'd grimly 'midst his courtier crew,
Who, gentle courtiers! all look'd *grimly* too!
Thus when in black the lofty SKY looks down,
The sympathizing SEA reflects a frown;
Vale, cattle, reptile, infect, man and maid,
All mope, and seem to sorrow in the shade.

Steep is th' ascent, and narrow is the road,
Ah me! that leads to Fame's divine abode:
Yet thick (through lanes, like pilgrimaging rats,
Unaw'd by mortals, and unscar'd by cats)
What crawling hosts attempt her sacred fane,
And dizzy, drunk-like, tumble back again;

Fast

Fast as the swains, whose arms the damsels fill,

Embrace of elegance down Greenwich Hill;

Whilst thou, Briareus like, with dauntless air,

Resolv'd to ravish FAME, immortal Fair;

Just like our London bullies with the w⸺,

Hast scal'd the cloud-capt height and forc'd her doors!

O form'd the trav'lers of the east to scare,

Although thy pow'rs are mighty, learn to spare:

Dog should not prey on dog, the proverb says:

Allow then brother-trav'lers crumbs of praise;

Like thee, let others reap applause and rise

By daring visits to Egyptian skies:

But calmly, lo! thou canst not see them pass;

" This is a rogue or fool, and that's an ass:"

Thus on a tree, whene'er the weather's fine,

JACK KETCH, the SPIDER, weaves the fatal line;

Beneath

Beneath a leaf he hides with watchful eye,
Now darts, and roping hangs the trav'ling FLY.
Again, moſt tireſome, let me ſay, Go, go,
Proceed, and *all about it* let us know:
Led ſafely by thine enterpriſing ſtar,
Hyenas ſhall not with thy journey war:
Uneat by tygers, dare the foreſt's gloom,
To bid the barren field of knowledge bloom:
Wave o'er new pyramids thine eagle wings;
And, hound-like, ſcent freſh tombs of ancient kings,
Which Time had buried with the mighty dead,
And cold Oblivion ſwallow'd in her ſhade:
And mind, 'tis HIST'RY's province to *ſurprize*;
That tales are ſweeteſt, that found moſt like lies.

F I N I S.

As the confessed superiority of Mr. BRUCE *to Mr.* BOSWELL *entitles him to a more eminent mark of distinction, I have added an* ODE, *in my best Manner, to this* Complimentary Epistle, *which the* Congratulatory Epistle to Mr. Boswell *cannot boast.*

ODE to JAMES BRUCE, Esq.

O BRUCE, for this his short and sweet epistle,
Thou biddest p'rhaps the gentle bard " go whistle;"
  Or somewhat worse, *perchaunce,* that rhimes to knight;
That is to say, knights of the blade,
One time so busy in the dubbing trade,
  That, like to silver, it was shoulder'd bright.

Pity by hungry critics thou shouldst fall,
So clever, and so form'd, to please us all!
        Again!

Again!—by royal favour all-surrounded,

A balm so rich, like cloves and nutmegs pounded!

Thus the BAG FOX, (how cruelly, alack!)

Turn'd out with turpentine upon his back,

Amidst the war of hounds and hunters flies;

Shows sport; but, luckless, by his fragrance dies!

Safe from the fury of the critic hounds,

O BRUCE, thou treadest Abyssinian grounds;

 Nor can our British noses hunt thy foil:

Indeed, thou need'st not dread th' event;

Surrounding clouds destroy the scent,

 And mock their most sagacious toil:

Yes, in thy darkness thou shalt leave the dogs;

For hares, the hunters say, run best in fogs.

Of thee and me, two great phyficians,

How diff'rent are the difpofitions!

 Thy foul delights in wonder, pomp, and buftle;

Mine in th' *un*marvellous and placid fcene,

Plain as the * hut of our good King and Queen;—

 I imitate the ftationary mufcle.

Yet, boldly thou, O BRUCE, again proceed;

Of wonder ope the fountain head;

 Deluge the land with Abyffinian ware;

Whilft I, a fimple fon of peace,

The world of *bagatelle* increafe,

 By love-fick fonnets to the fair:

* A houfe clofe by the glorious caftle of Windfor.

Now to Sir Joseph, now a Duke, now Wren,
Now Robin Red-breast, dedicate the pen;
　Now Glow-worm, child of shade and light, not flame;
To whom, of wicked wits, the tuneful art,
So very apt, indeed, from truth to start,
　Compares the nightly street-meand'ring dame.

Mild INSECT, harmless as myself, I ween;
Thou little planet of the rural scene,
When summer warms the vallies with her rays;
Accept a trifling sonnet to thy praise.

ODE to the GLOW-WORM.

BRIGHT stranger, welcome to my field,
Here feed in safety, here thy radiance yield;
 To me, O nightly be thy splendor giv'n:
O could a wish of mine the skies command,
How would I gem thy leaf with lib'ral hand,
 With ev'ry sweetest dew of Heav'n!

Say, dost thou kindly light the Fairy train,
Amidst their gambols on the stilly plain,
 Hanging thy lamp upon the moisten'd blade?
What lamp so fit, so pure as thine,
Amidst the gentle elfin band to shine,
 And chace the horrors of the midnight shade!

Oh! may no feather'd foe disturb thy bow'r,
And with barbarian beak thy life devour:
   Oh! may no ruthless torrent of the sky,
O'erwhelming, force thee from thy dewy seat;
Nor tempests tear thee from thy green retreat,
   And bid thee midst the humming myriads die.

Queen of the insect world, what leaves delight?
   Of such these willing hands a bow'r shall form,
To guard thee from the rushing rains of night,
   And hide thee from the wild wing of the storm.

Sweet Child of Stillness, midst the awful calm
   Of pausing Nature thou art pleas'd to dwell;
In happy silence to enjoy thy balm,
   And shed through life a lustre round thy cell.

How

How diff'rent man, the imp of noise and strife,

Who courts the storm that tears and darkens life;

Blest when the passions wild the soul invade!

How nobler far to bid those whirlwinds cease;

To taste, like thee, the luxury of peace,

And shine in solitude and shade!

ERRATA.

Page 3, line 14—For *make*, read *wash*.
10, line 10—For *their*, read *your*.
13, line 4—For *had*, read *has*.
line 8—For a *period*, put a *semicolon*.
10, line 8—For *her*, read *the*.

A LIST of PETER PINDAR's WORKS;

Any of which may be had of G. KEARSLEY, No. 46, Fleet-Street, and the Country Bookfellers.

	l.	s.	d.
1. A Supplicating EPISTLE to the REVIEWERS,	0	1	6
2. LYRIC ODES to the Royal Academicians, for 1782,	0	2	0
3. ———————————————————— 1783,	0	1	6
4. ———————————————————— 1785,	0	2	6
5. FAREWELL ODES, —————— 1786,	0	3	0
6. The LOUSIAD, Canto I.	0	2	6
7. ——————— Canto II.	0	2	6
8. Congratulatory EPISTLE to JAMES BOSWELL,	0	2	0
9. BOZZI and PIOZZI, a TOWN ECLOGUE,	0	3	0
10. ODE upon ODE, or a PEEP at St. JAMES's,	0	3	0
11. An Apologetic POSTCRIPT to ODE upon ODE,	0	1	6
12. INSTRUCTIONS to a certain POET LAUREAT,	0	2	6
13. BROTHER PETER to BROTHER TOM,	0	3	0
14. PETER's PENSION, a Solemn EPISTLE,	0	3	0
15. PETER's PROPHECY,	0	3	0
16. Sir J. BANKS and the EMPEROR of MOROCCO,	0	1	6
17. EPISTLE to a FALLING MINISTER,	0	2	6
18. SUBJECTS for PAINTERS,	0	3	6
19. EXPOSTULATORY ODES to a Great DUKE and a Little LORD	0	2	6
20. BENEVOLENT EPISTLE to NICHOLS,	0	2	6
21. ODE to the Future LAUREAT,	0	1	6
22. EPISTLE to BRUCE,	0	2	6
	2	13	0

⁂ Complete Sets may now be had, including a Mezzotinto Engraving of the Author by one of our most eminent Artists.

N. B. The complete Set, WITHOUT the Portrait of the Author, is spurious.

www.ingramcontent.com/pod-product-compliance
Lightning Source LLC
Chambersburg PA
CBHW030710110426
42739CB00031B/1537